EMMANUEL JOSEPH

The Cosmic Psyche, Exploring the Universe Through Literature and the Human Mind

Copyright © 2025 by Emmanuel Joseph

All rights reserved. No part of this publication may be reproduced, stored or transmitted in any form or by any means, electronic, mechanical, photocopying, recording, scanning, or otherwise without written permission from the publisher. It is illegal to copy this book, post it to a website, or distribute it by any other means without permission.

First edition

This book was professionally typeset on Reedsy.
Find out more at reedsy.com

Contents

1	Chapter 1: The Dawn of Cosmic Consciousness	1
2	Chapter 2: Myth and Mystery	3
3	Chapter 3: The Scientific Revolution	5
4	Chapter 4: Cosmic Horror and Existentialism	7
5	Chapter 5: The Interstellar Frontier	9
6	Chapter 6: The Quest for Extraterrestrial Life	11
7	Chapter 7: The Cosmic Landscape	13
8	Chapter 8: The Cosmic Mind	15
9	Chapter 9: The Cosmic Journey	17
10	Chapter 10: The Cosmic Paradox	19
11	Chapter 11: The Cosmic Symphony	21
12	Chapter 12: The Cosmic Future	23
13	Chapter 13: The Cosmic Arts	24
14	Chapter 14: The Cosmic Legacy	26
15	Chapter 15: The Cosmic Connection	28

1

Chapter 1: The Dawn of Cosmic Consciousness

In the beginning, human beings gazed at the night sky, mesmerized by its infinite expanse and twinkling stars. This awe inspired stories and myths, creating a rich tapestry of cosmic narratives that transcended generations. The stars became symbols of hope, mystery, and adventure, embedding themselves deeply into the human psyche. Ancient civilizations used constellations to navigate and predict events, establishing a profound connection between the cosmos and human existence.

As our understanding of the universe grew, so did our literary explorations. Early astronomers like Ptolemy and Copernicus laid the groundwork for cosmic understanding, which in turn influenced writers and philosophers. Literature became a medium to explore the mysteries of the universe, reflecting our evolving comprehension and curiosity. Stories of celestial journeys and encounters with otherworldly beings flourished, blending science and imagination.

In modern times, literature continues to be a powerful tool for exploring cosmic themes. Science fiction, in particular, has become a genre where writers speculate about the future and the unknown. Authors like Isaac Asimov and Arthur C. Clarke have expanded our cosmic consciousness, challenging us to ponder the possibilities of life beyond Earth. Through their works, we envision new worlds and question our place in the vast cosmos.

The relationship between literature and the cosmos is a testament to the human desire to understand and connect with the universe. By weaving cosmic elements into stories, writers help us grapple with existential questions and inspire us to look beyond the horizon. The cosmic psyche is a reflection of our innate curiosity and the timeless quest for knowledge and meaning in an ever-expanding universe.

2

Chapter 2: Myth and Mystery

Mythology has always played a crucial role in shaping our understanding of the cosmos. Ancient cultures created elaborate stories to explain the origins of the universe and the forces that govern it. These myths were not just explanations; they were expressions of wonder and reverence for the mysteries of existence. The stars and planets were often personified as gods and goddesses, each with their own stories and significance.

In Greek mythology, the cosmos was a living entity, with deities like Zeus and Hera reigning over the heavens. The constellations told tales of heroes and monsters, serving as celestial reminders of human virtues and vices. These myths were more than entertainment; they were a means of connecting with the divine and understanding the natural world. The stories were passed down through generations, preserving cultural heritage and cosmic knowledge.

Similarly, Native American tribes viewed the cosmos as a sacred space, filled with spirits and ancestors. The stars were seen as guides and protectors, with each constellation holding unique meaning and power. These celestial narratives were integral to their spiritual beliefs and practices, reinforcing the connection between the earth and the sky. The myths were not static; they evolved with the people, adapting to new understandings and experiences.

Modern literature continues to draw inspiration from these ancient myths, reinterpreting them for contemporary audiences. Writers like Neil Gaiman and Rick Riordan have revitalized mythology, blending it with modern storytelling techniques. By doing so, they keep the cosmic mysteries alive, inviting readers to explore the unknown and embrace the wonder of the universe. The enduring appeal of myth is a testament to its power to capture the imagination and connect us to the cosmos.

3

Chapter 3: The Scientific Revolution

The Scientific Revolution marked a turning point in our understanding of the universe. With the advent of the telescope, astronomers like Galileo and Kepler made groundbreaking discoveries that challenged existing beliefs. These advancements were not just scientific; they had profound implications for literature and the human psyche. The cosmos was no longer a realm of myths and legends but a subject of empirical study and exploration.

Literature of the period reflected this shift, with writers incorporating scientific discoveries into their works. John Milton's "Paradise Lost" explored the grandeur of the cosmos, blending poetic imagination with astronomical knowledge. The universe was portrayed as a dynamic and awe-inspiring space, filled with celestial wonders and divine mysteries. This fusion of science and literature enriched the human experience, fostering a deeper connection to the cosmos.

As the scientific community continued to unravel the secrets of the universe, literature evolved alongside it. The Enlightenment era saw a surge in scientific writings and speculative fiction. Authors like Mary Shelley and Jonathan Swift used their works to explore the ethical and philosophical implications of scientific advancements. The cosmos became a canvas for examining human nature and societal progress, raising questions about the future and our place in the universe.

Today, the legacy of the Scientific Revolution lives on in literature. Science fiction writers continue to push the boundaries of imagination, envisioning new technologies and cosmic scenarios. The genre serves as a bridge between scientific inquiry and creative expression, allowing readers to explore the possibilities of the future. The fusion of science and literature is a testament to the enduring human desire to understand the cosmos and our role within it.

4

Chapter 4: Cosmic Horror and Existentialism

The vastness and mystery of the cosmos have also inspired darker themes in literature. Cosmic horror, a subgenre popularized by writers like H.P. Lovecraft, delves into the fear and awe of the unknown. The universe is depicted as indifferent and incomprehensible, filled with ancient, malevolent entities that defy human understanding. This genre taps into existential anxieties, questioning our significance in the grand scheme of things.

Lovecraft's works, such as "The Call of Cthulhu," explore the terror of cosmic insignificance. His protagonists often encounter entities that shatter their perception of reality, leading to madness and despair. These stories reflect a deep-seated fear of the unknown and the limits of human knowledge. The cosmos is portrayed as a hostile and indifferent space, where humanity is but a fleeting speck in an uncaring universe.

Existentialist writers like Albert Camus and Jean-Paul Sartre also grappled with these themes, albeit from a philosophical perspective. They questioned the meaning of life in an indifferent universe, exploring the tension between human aspirations and cosmic indifference. Literature became a means of confronting existential dilemmas, offering a space to reflect on the human condition and our place in the cosmos.

Modern writers continue to explore cosmic horror and existentialism, blending these themes with contemporary issues. Works by authors like Jeff VanderMeer and Thomas Ligotti push the boundaries of the genre, delving into the psychological and philosophical implications of cosmic dread. These stories challenge readers to confront their fears and grapple with the unknown, reflecting the enduring power of the cosmos to evoke awe and terror.

5

Chapter 5: The Interstellar Frontier

The idea of exploring the cosmos has always captivated human imagination. From early myths of celestial voyages to modern space exploration, the dream of traversing the stars has driven both scientific and literary endeavors. The interstellar frontier represents the ultimate quest for knowledge and adventure, a symbol of humanity's insatiable curiosity and desire to push beyond the known.

Literature has played a crucial role in shaping our vision of space exploration. Jules Verne's "From the Earth to the Moon" and H.G. Wells' "The War of the Worlds" envisioned journeys to other planets and encounters with extraterrestrial beings. These stories ignited the imaginations of readers, inspiring generations of scientists and explorers to turn fiction into reality. The interstellar frontier became a space where the boundaries between science and imagination blurred.

As humanity began to venture into space, literature evolved to reflect these new possibilities. The Space Age gave rise to a new wave of science fiction, with writers like Arthur C. Clarke and Robert A. Heinlein exploring the challenges and triumphs of interstellar travel. Their works delved into the technical, ethical, and emotional aspects of space exploration, offering a glimpse into the future of humanity among the stars.

Today, the interstellar frontier continues to inspire writers and readers alike. Science fiction serves as a speculative laboratory, where authors envision new technologies and societal structures that may arise from space exploration. The genre challenges us to consider the implications of venturing beyond Earth, reflecting our hopes, fears, and aspirations. The interstellar frontier is a testament to the enduring power of the cosmos to captivate and inspire the human mind.

6

Chapter 6: The Quest for Extraterrestrial Life

The search for extraterrestrial life has long been a focal point of both scientific inquiry and literary imagination. The possibility of life beyond Earth raises profound questions about our place in the universe and the nature of life itself. Literature has explored these themes in diverse and imaginative ways, envisioning encounters with alien civilizations and the implications of such discoveries.

In the early days of science fiction, writers like H.G. Wells and Edgar Rice Burroughs speculated about life on Mars and other planets. These stories reflected contemporary scientific theories and popular fascination with the possibility of extraterrestrial beings. The concept of intelligent life beyond Earth sparked the imaginations of readers, fueling a sense of wonder and curiosity about the cosmos.

As our understanding of the universe expanded, so did the complexity of literary explorations of extraterrestrial life. Authors like Philip K. Dick and Ursula K. Le Guin delved into the ethical and philosophical implications of encountering alien civilizations. Their works raised questions about identity, communication, and the nature of consciousness, challenging readers to think beyond anthropocentric perspectives.

Today, the search for extraterrestrial life continues to inspire writers and scientists alike. The discovery of exoplanets and advancements in astrobiology have opened new possibilities for imagining life beyond Earth. Contemporary science fiction explores these themes with greater nuance and sophistication, envisioning a diverse array of alien species and ecosystems. The quest for extraterrestrial life remains a powerful symbol of humanity's desire to understand the universe and our place within it.

7

Chapter 7: The Cosmic Landscape

The cosmos is a vast and ever-changing landscape, filled with celestial wonders and mysteries waiting to be discovered. From the swirling nebulae to the distant galaxies, the universe offers a limitless canvas for human imagination. Literature has long sought to capture the beauty and complexity of the cosmic landscape, blending scientific knowledge with poetic expression.

Early astronomers like Johannes Kepler and Tycho Brahe were among the first to meticulously chart the stars and planets, bridging the gap between observation and imagination. Their work laid the foundation for a deeper understanding of the cosmos and inspired countless literary explorations. The cosmic landscape became a source of endless fascination, with writers attempting to capture its grandeur and mystery through words.

In modern literature, the beauty of the cosmos is often depicted through vivid descriptions and poetic language. Authors like Carl Sagan and Ann Druyan have translated scientific knowledge into accessible and awe-inspiring prose, bringing the wonders of the universe to a broader audience. Their works blend rigorous scientific inquiry with a profound sense of wonder, inviting readers to explore the cosmos with a sense of curiosity and reverence.

The cosmic landscape also serves as a metaphor for the human experience. The vastness of the universe mirrors the complexity of the human mind, with its countless thoughts, emotions, and dreams. Literature often uses celestial imagery to explore themes of love, loss, and longing, drawing parallels between the boundless expanse of the cosmos and the depths of the human soul. This interplay between the cosmic and the personal enriches our understanding of both, creating a tapestry of meaning that transcends the boundaries of space and time.

As we continue to explore the universe, the cosmic landscape will remain a powerful source of inspiration for writers and artists. The ever-changing nature of the cosmos offers endless possibilities for creative expression, encouraging us to look beyond the familiar and embrace the unknown. The cosmic landscape is not just a backdrop for stories; it is a living, breathing entity that reflects our innermost thoughts and aspirations, inviting us to journey into the depths of our imagination and beyond.

8

Chapter 8: The Cosmic Mind

The concept of the cosmic mind, or the idea that the universe itself possesses consciousness, has intrigued philosophers and writers for centuries. This notion challenges conventional understandings of mind and matter, suggesting that the cosmos is more than just a collection of physical objects—it is a living, thinking entity. Literature has explored this idea in various forms, blending science, philosophy, and spirituality to create a rich tapestry of cosmic thought.

In ancient texts, the idea of a cosmic mind was often linked to divine beings or universal consciousness. Hindu and Buddhist philosophies, for example, speak of the universe as a manifestation of a higher consciousness, where all beings are interconnected. These concepts found their way into literature, shaping narratives that emphasized the unity of all existence and the interconnectedness of the cosmos.

In the 20th century, the concept of the cosmic mind gained renewed interest through the works of writers like Teilhard de Chardin and Carl Jung. They proposed that human consciousness is a reflection of a greater cosmic intelligence, suggesting that our minds are part of a vast, interconnected web of awareness. This idea resonated with readers, offering a new perspective on the nature of consciousness and our place in the universe.

Contemporary literature continues to explore the concept of the cosmic mind, blending scientific discoveries with philosophical insights. Writers like Philip K. Dick and Olaf Stapledon have envisioned futures where humanity merges with cosmic consciousness, exploring the implications of such transformations. These stories challenge readers to consider the nature of mind and matter, inviting us to ponder the mysteries of existence and our connection to the cosmos.

9

Chapter 9: The Cosmic Journey

The theme of the cosmic journey has been a cornerstone of literature for centuries. From epic quests to interstellar voyages, these narratives reflect humanity's enduring desire to explore the unknown and push the boundaries of what is possible. The cosmic journey symbolizes the quest for knowledge, adventure, and self-discovery, capturing the imagination of readers and inspiring generations of explorers and dreamers.

In classical literature, cosmic journeys often took the form of mythological quests. Heroes like Odysseus and Gilgamesh ventured into uncharted realms, facing challenges and discovering new truths about themselves and the world. These stories resonated with audiences, reflecting the human spirit of exploration and the desire to understand the cosmos and our place within it.

As our understanding of the universe expanded, so did the scope of cosmic journeys in literature. The advent of space exploration inspired a new wave of science fiction, with writers envisioning journeys to distant planets and galaxies. Works like Frank Herbert's "Dune" and Isaac Asimov's "Foundation" series explored the political, social, and ethical dimensions of interstellar travel, offering readers a glimpse into the future of humanity among the stars.

Today, the cosmic journey continues to be a powerful narrative theme. Modern science fiction writers blend cutting-edge scientific concepts with imaginative storytelling, creating rich and diverse visions of the future. These stories challenge us to consider the possibilities of space exploration and the implications for humanity, inviting us to embark on our own cosmic journeys of discovery and adventure.

10

Chapter 10: The Cosmic Paradox

The universe is filled with paradoxes that challenge our understanding of reality. From the nature of time and space to the existence of parallel universes, these cosmic mysteries have inspired countless literary explorations. The cosmic paradox invites us to question the boundaries of knowledge and embrace the unknown, offering a space for imaginative and philosophical inquiry.

One of the most intriguing cosmic paradoxes is the nature of time. Literature has long explored the complexities of time travel, with authors like H.G. Wells and Ray Bradbury envisioning journeys to the past and future. These stories reflect our fascination with the malleability of time and the potential for altering the course of history. The cosmic paradox of time challenges us to consider the implications of our actions and the interconnectedness of past, present, and future.

Another compelling cosmic paradox is the concept of parallel universes. The idea that multiple realities exist simultaneously has been a staple of science fiction, with writers like Philip K. Dick and Stephen King exploring the possibilities of alternate worlds. These narratives invite readers to question the nature of reality and consider the infinite possibilities of existence. The cosmic paradox of parallel universes offers a space for creative and philosophical exploration, challenging us to expand our understanding of the cosmos.

The cosmic paradox also extends to the nature of existence itself. The question of whether the universe is finite or infinite has long puzzled scientists and philosophers. Literature provides a space to explore these mysteries, blending scientific inquiry with imaginative speculation. Writers like Jorge Luis Borges and Italo Calvino have used their works to delve into the paradoxes of existence, offering readers a glimpse into the profound mysteries of the cosmos.

11

Chapter 11: The Cosmic Symphony

The universe is often described as a cosmic symphony, with celestial bodies moving in harmony and cosmic forces interacting in a delicate balance. This metaphor captures the beauty and complexity of the cosmos, inviting us to see the universe as a work of art. Literature has long used musical imagery to describe the cosmos, blending science and art to create a rich and evocative tapestry of cosmic harmony.

In ancient texts, the music of the spheres was a common metaphor for the harmony of the cosmos. Philosophers like Pythagoras and Plato believed that the movements of celestial bodies produced a divine music, reflecting the order and beauty of the universe. This idea found its way into literature, shaping narratives that emphasized the interconnectedness of all things and the harmony of the cosmos.

In modern literature, the cosmic symphony is often used to describe the intricate patterns and rhythms of the universe. Authors like James Joyce and Virginia Woolf have used musical language to convey the flow of time and the interconnectedness of human experiences. The cosmic symphony serves as a metaphor for the complexity and beauty of existence, inviting readers to see the universe as a living, breathing entity.

The metaphor of the cosmic symphony also extends to our understanding of the natural world. The rhythms of the seasons, the cycles of life and death, and the patterns of the stars all reflect the harmony of the cosmos.

Literature captures these rhythms, blending scientific observation with poetic expression to create a rich and immersive portrayal of the natural world. The cosmic symphony invites us to see the universe as a work of art, filled with beauty and meaning.

12

Chapter 12: The Cosmic Future

As we look to the future, the cosmos continues to inspire our dreams and aspirations. The possibilities of space exploration, the search for extraterrestrial life, and the quest for knowledge drive us to push the boundaries of what is possible. Literature plays a crucial role in shaping our vision of the cosmic future, offering a space to imagine new worlds and consider the implications of our actions.

Contemporary science fiction writers are at the forefront of envisioning the cosmic future. Authors like Kim Stanley Robinson and Liu Cixin explore the challenges and triumphs of space colonization, imagining the future of humanity among the stars. Their works raise important questions about the ethics of exploration, the impact of technology, and the future of human society. The cosmic future is a space for speculative inquiry, inviting readers to consider the possibilities of the unknown.

The search for extraterrestrial life also continues to drive our cosmic aspirations. The discovery of microbial life on Mars or intelligent civilizations in distant galaxies would have profound implications for our understanding of the universe and our place within it. Literature explores these possibilities, blending scientific inquiry with imaginative storytelling to create rich and diverse visions of the future. The cosmic future invites us to consider the implications of these discoveries and reflect on the nature of existence.

13

Chapter 13: The Cosmic Arts

The cosmos has long served as a muse for artists, inspiring works that capture the beauty and mystery of the universe. From celestial paintings to space-themed music, the cosmic arts encompass a diverse array of creative expressions that reflect our fascination with the stars. These artistic endeavors offer a unique perspective on the cosmos, blending scientific knowledge with imaginative interpretation.

In the visual arts, the cosmos has been depicted in various forms, from the starry night skies of Van Gogh to the surreal space landscapes of contemporary artists. These works invite viewers to contemplate the vastness and wonder of the universe, evoking a sense of awe and curiosity. The cosmic arts also extend to architecture, with structures like observatories and planetariums designed to bring the cosmos closer to us.

Music, too, has been deeply influenced by the cosmos. Composers like Gustav Holst and John Williams have created iconic pieces that capture the grandeur and mystery of space. The cosmic arts offer a way to explore the universe through sound, evoking the emotions and sensations of celestial journeys. Literature often incorporates these musical elements, blending words and melodies to create rich and immersive experiences.

The cosmic arts also include digital and interactive media, with artists using technology to create immersive experiences that transport audiences to the stars. Virtual reality, for example, allows users to explore distant galaxies and celestial phenomena, bridging the gap between imagination and reality. These innovative forms of expression invite us to see the cosmos in new and exciting ways, expanding our understanding and appreciation of the universe.

14

Chapter 14: The Cosmic Legacy

The legacy of cosmic exploration and imagination is a testament to humanity's enduring quest for knowledge and understanding. From ancient myths to modern scientific discoveries, the stories we tell about the cosmos reflect our evolving relationship with the universe. The cosmic legacy is a rich tapestry of cultural, scientific, and artistic achievements that inspire and guide us as we journey into the future.

One of the most enduring aspects of the cosmic legacy is the knowledge passed down through generations. Ancient astronomers like Ptolemy and Copernicus laid the groundwork for our understanding of the cosmos, inspiring future scientists and explorers. Their discoveries were not just scientific milestones; they were cultural touchstones that shaped our perception of the universe and our place within it.

The cosmic legacy also includes the stories and myths that have been told and retold throughout history. These narratives offer a window into the human psyche, revealing our hopes, fears, and aspirations. Literature preserves these stories, ensuring that the wisdom and wonder of the cosmos are passed down to future generations. The cosmic legacy is a reminder of our shared humanity and our collective journey through the stars.

As we continue to explore the universe, the cosmic legacy will evolve, incorporating new discoveries and insights. The stories we tell today will become part of this legacy, inspiring future generations to look to the stars

CHAPTER 14: THE COSMIC LEGACY

and dream of what lies beyond. The cosmic legacy is a testament to the enduring power of the cosmos to captivate and inspire the human mind, inviting us to continue our journey of exploration and discovery.

15

Chapter 15: The Cosmic Connection

At the heart of our fascination with the cosmos is the profound sense of connection it inspires. The stars and galaxies are not just distant objects; they are part of a vast, interconnected web of existence that includes us. The cosmic connection is a reminder of our place in the universe and the bonds that unite all things. Literature explores this connection, blending science, philosophy, and spirituality to create a rich and evocative tapestry of meaning.

The concept of the cosmic connection is deeply rooted in ancient philosophies and spiritual traditions. Indigenous cultures around the world have long viewed the cosmos as a sacred space, filled with spirits and ancestors. These beliefs emphasize the interconnectedness of all things and the importance of living in harmony with the natural world. Literature preserves these wisdoms, offering a space to explore the cosmic connection and its implications for our lives.

In modern times, the cosmic connection has been explored through the lens of science and technology. The discovery of the interconnectedness of ecosystems and the delicate balance of the Earth's climate are reminders of our place within the larger cosmic web. Literature reflects these insights, blending scientific knowledge with imaginative storytelling to create a rich and nuanced understanding of the cosmic connection.

The cosmic connection also extends to our relationships with each other.

CHAPTER 15: THE COSMIC CONNECTION

The stories we tell about the cosmos are a reflection of our shared humanity and our collective journey through the stars. Literature offers a space to explore the bonds that unite us, transcending the boundaries of time and space. The cosmic connection is a reminder of our shared journey and the enduring power of the cosmos to inspire and connect us.

Book Description:

The Cosmic Psyche, Exploring the Universe Through Literature and the Human Mind takes readers on a mesmerizing journey through the vast expanse of the cosmos and the rich depths of human imagination. This captivating book weaves together science, mythology, philosophy, and art to explore the profound connection between the universe and the human psyche. Through twelve insightful chapters, readers will delve into the dawn of cosmic consciousness, the enduring allure of myths and mysteries, the transformative power of the scientific revolution, and the dark allure of cosmic horror and existentialism.

With eloquent prose and vivid storytelling, *The Cosmic Psyche* invites readers to explore the interstellar frontier, ponder the quest for extraterrestrial life, and marvel at the intricate beauty of the cosmic landscape. The book also delves into the concept of the cosmic mind, the enduring appeal of cosmic journeys, and the paradoxes that challenge our understanding of reality. Through the cosmic symphony of celestial movements and the legacy of cosmic exploration, readers will discover the profound sense of connection that unites all things.

Richly illustrated and deeply thought-provoking, *The Cosmic Psyche* is a celebration of the human spirit's insatiable curiosity and the timeless quest for knowledge and meaning. Whether you are a lover of science fiction, a student of philosophy, or simply a curious soul, this book will inspire you to look to the stars and embrace the wonder of the universe.

www.ingramcontent.com/pod-product-compliance
Lightning Source LLC
LaVergne TN
LVHW020740090526
838202LV00057BA/6155